MAKI'S BUSY WEEK

Linda Hinchliffe

AN OMF BOOK

MONDAY

It was breakfast time at Maki's house. Mum had some plates spread in a line and was lifting the big cooking pot off the hook over the fireplace. She took the lid off the pot and Maki could see their breakfast steaming inside the pot.

"Oh good, rice and potatoes!" said Maki. "We're hungry, aren't we Tanga?"

"Tanga hungry tatoes!" said Tanga. Maki smiled. It was fun now that his little sister was starting to talk. Sometimes she said the words a bit wrong and made his dad and mum laugh.

"Call for your dad and Juni," said mum. "They are outside in the yard."

Maki looked out of the doorway into the yard. His dad and his big brother Juni were chasing a small pig out of the garden.

"Dad!" shouted Maki. His dad looked round.

"Hi Maki," he said. "Is it time for breakfast in there yet?"

"Yes, mum says to come now," said Maki.

Maki's dad and Juni came inside and all of them sat down around the plates. On each plate mum had put a pile of rice and some potatoes. Just one small potato for Tanga, two for Maki, three for Juni and five each for dad and herself. They all started to eat.

"The only trouble with this breakfast is that there is no

vegetable soup to make it juicy," said Juni.

"I know, Juni," said mum. "The ducks and pigs always come and eat our vegetables before they can grow big. Like that small pig you chased away just before you came inside."

"Maybe you and I had better go and cut bamboo poles this morning," said dad to Juni.

"Why, will we eat bamboo poles?" asked Maki.

"Silly!" said Juni. "Even animals don't eat bamboo poles."

"Well, what are the bamboo poles for then?" asked Maki.

"For a fence," said dad. "We'll make a fence all around our garden. Then the straying pigs won't be able to get near our plants."

"We'll have something tasty to eat with our rice and potatoes every day!" said Juni.

"I want to help make the fence too!" said Maki.

After breakfast, dad and Juni went off to cut long bamboo poles. Soon they were back, carrying the poles on their shoulders. They laid them down on the ground.

"Pity geen!" said Tanga.

"Yes, they are a pretty green colour," said Maki. The children went over and touched the poles. They were very smooth, and cold too.

"Clack, clack, clack." Dad started to chop one of the poles. The children sat on the house steps and watched. Maki knew that dad's knife was very sharp. He and Tanga needed to stay out of the way.

"Clack, clack, clack," went the knife. Soon there were lots of short poles. Then dad started to slice the poles down the middle.

"Slish, slish, slish," went his knife. Inside the bamboo poles were white coloured.

"Slish, slish," dad went on slicing. Maki made a rhyme and told it to Tanga:

"Slish, slish, green and white sticks.

Slish, slish, green and white sticks."

They both liked watching the sticks fall as dad cut them. Soon there were lots of sticks.

Then dad and Juni began to push the sticks in the ground to make a fence.

Maki saw the ends of the bamboo poles that were too short for fence sticks. He picked them up and laid them on the ground under the stepladder.

"We'll make a playhouse," he told Tanga. "This can be our floor." Tanga sat on their new floor.

Then Maki borrowed some of the tall sticks from his dad's pile.

"These can be our houseposts," he told Tanga. He pushed them in the ground at each corner of the floor.

Then Maki found a giant sized leaf at the side of the garden. "This can be our roof," he told Tanga. He balanced the leaf on top of the posts. Then he sat under the leaf roof next to Tanga.

"Nice oof!" said Tanga, pointing up at the roof. She smiled. She liked their playhouse.

Suddenly they heard a voice calling outside.

"Hello! May I visit you in your playhouse, children?" said the voice.

They looked out, but the leaf roof dropped down so much that they could see only legs. Legs that were white, not brown like theirs. It must be Mam the missionary!

Tanga let out a cry and hid her face against Maki's shirt. She was scared of Mam.

"Don't be scared," Maki told her.

When Mam was new in the village, Maki had been scared of her too, just like Tanga was now. Why, not just her legs but her whole body was white. She was bigger and taller than any of the mums and dads too. But she was friendly and had learnt to speak their language. Maki wasn't scared of her any more.

"Where is the doorway?" It was Mam's voice again. They could see her face now as she peered through the stepladder and underneath the leaf to see them.

Maki started to laugh. "You can't come inside. It's too small in here. It's only for children!" he told Mam. Then Tanga started to laugh too. She wasn't scared of Mam any more.

Just then Maki's mum climbed down the stepladder. She and Mam started talking together.

Maki heard his dad calling from the far corner of the garden. "Maki, you can help us now by carrying piles of sticks over to us. We will push them in the ground."

So Maki carried piles of sticks. Even Tanga helped too. She carried one stick in each hand.

"What do you think?" asked dad. "Could even the smallest pig squeeze through our fence?"

"Oh no," said Maki. "Not even a tiny duck will be able to squeeze through when we have finished."

"Our vegetables will be able to grow very big now!" said Juni.

"Tanga big now," said Tanga.

"Yes, you are big now!" said mum. "And you will grow even bigger. All of you will, when you have lots of vegetables to eat every day."

TUESDAY

Maki heard a noise up in the sky. "Nuu nuu ..." It was a plane. He ran to his friend, Sami. He played with Sami almost every day. They both saw the plane high up in the sky.

"Let's be planes," said Maki.

"Oh yes, let's be planes," said Sami.

"Nuu nuu ..." said the children. They held out their arms and ran down the path as fast as they could.

They were saying "Nuu nuu ..." very loud and running very fast when they saw Juni. He was sitting at the side of the path. He was very busy making something.

"What are you making, Juni?" Maki asked his big brother.

"I'm making a toy plane," said Juni. "Be careful! Don't grab at it like that!"

Maki and Sami watched quietly as Juni tried to fix the wings onto the body of the plane. It was hard to do.

"The wings won't stay in place," said Juni. "They fall off again every time I fix them."

Maki had an idea. "Let's go and ask Mam the missionary how to do it," he said. "Mam knows all about planes."

"Oh yes," said Sami. "Let's go and ask Mam. She rode in a plane when she came to our country. I heard her telling my dad about it."

"Huh! You little kids. Don't be silly. Just because she rode in a real plane doesn't mean she'll know how to fix a toy one!" Juni kept trying to fix the wings onto the body of the plane, but they fell off every time.

At last he said, "Well, I suppose we could ask Mam the missionary. She might have string I could tie the wings on with."

Juni picked up the pieces of the plane and the children walked along the path to the missionary's house. Mam came outside when the children got to her step ladder.

"Hello, children," she said.

"We need some of your string," said Maki.

"Maki, be quiet!" said Juni and Sami. But it was all right because Mam was smiling.

"What do you need the string for?" she asked the children.

"It's for Juni's toy plane, Mam," said Sami.

"It won't work because the wings won't stay in place," said Juni.

Mam went inside the house and came back with some pink string. Juni quickly tied the wings onto the body of his plane. Then he fixed it onto a long thin bamboo pole. Now it was ready to fly.

Maki and Sami looked up into the air while Juni tested out the plane. He held the pole with both hands. The plane swayed up high in the air as the pole bent to and fro.

"It's almost like a real plane," said Maki and Sami. Mam said so too.

"Tell us about riding in a real plane, Mam," said Juni.

"Yes, tell us ... weren't you scared of falling out?" said Sami.

"Oh no," said Mam. "It's like going inside a house and then the door is shut. Then it starts to fly in the sky, and you don't fall out because there are no holes to fall out through. Anyway, I knew I was safe because God was looking after me. I wasn't scared."

The children were ready to run and play again.

"Bye Mam," they said as they set off running down the path. Juni ran in front holding the new toy plane on its long swaying pole. Maki and Sami ran behind saying "Nuu nuu ..." loudly again.

At home, Juni pushed the long bamboo pole into the ground outside the house. They all went up the step ladder and looked out of the window to watch the plane.

"Nuu nuu ... now it's swaying downwards, it's going to land," said Maki.

"Now it's going up again ... Nuu nuu," said Sami.

"It's scarey, but the people riding aren't scared. They know God is looking after them," said Juni. The children had lots of fun watching the plane.

When it was almost dark, Sami went home for his supper. Maki and Juni ate their supper too.

"Will you make a plane for me tomorrow, Juni?" said Maki. "One for Sami too?"

"All right," said Juni. "I'll make one for each of you, so long as Mam the missionary has some more string!"

Then Maki had another idea. "Let's be missionaries when we grow up," he said. "Then we can even ride in a real plane, just like Mam."

WEDNESDAY

"Oh, there you are, Maki," said his mum. "I was looking for you."

"I was flying my new plane," said Maki. "Juni made it for me. He made one for Sami too. We flew them around all the houses and back again."

"Well, I don't think your plane should go out flying this afternoon," said Maki's mum. "There will be a big rain. Stay near home. Then when the big rain comes you can run inside quickly."

Maki's mum was getting ready to go out. "Where are you going?" asked Maki.

"I am going to the reading class at Mam's house," said his mum.

"Let me come with you to the class!" said Maki. He liked going to Mam's house. There were books with coloured pictures of things he had never seen before. He would look at them while the ladies practised reading.

So Maki went with his mum to the class. Five other ladies were already sitting on the floor when they arrived. Each of them had a reading book, some paper and a pencil. One of them had her baby with her too.

The ladies enjoyed their class, but it was hard for them to learn. They had never had the chance to learn to read and write when they were small. They were no schools

then. Now that they were grown up, their minds had so many other things to think about every day.

"I just can't remember all these different shaped letters," said one lady. "All my mind knows is the shape of a potato!"

"Yes," said another lady. "That's the thing we women learn from being small. Potatoes. Planting them. Digging them up. Washing them. Carrying them. Cooking them."

"Will we ever be able to read the Bible books?" asked another lady.

"Oh yes," said Mam. "We just go slowly, learning a few letters each month. Soon you will know them all. Then you can read the Bible books. Maki's mum, you be the one to pray today."

Maki's mum prayed that God would help them to learn fast and remember the letters. Then the class began.

Mam wrote on the board with her white chalk. She

wrote the letter *a*. "You already know this letter," she said. "Let's all read it." All the ladies read "a."

Then Mam wrote the letter *u*. "You already know this letter too," she said. "Let's all read it." All the ladies read "u."

Then Mam wrote *da* on the board. "Now, who remembers what this says? First we write its potato-shaped body, then we give it a stem. Then we put its friend next to it." Mam wrote *da* again while she talked.

Maki's mum remembered what it said. "Da," she read.

"Good!" said Mam. Then Mam wrote *du* on the board. All the ladies read together, "a u da du."

Then Mam wrote something new on the board. She wrote *na*. "This is *na*," said Mam. Then she wrote *nu* on the board. "This is *nu*," she said.

All the ladies practised reading the new letter. "Na nu," they read. "a u da du na nu." Then they practised writing *na* and *nu*.

The ladies were working hard to write *na* and *nu*. They did not notice when the wind started to blow. The wind blew into the house. "Crash!" The blackboard fell over flat on its face on the floor. Then papers began to fly down from the shelf above the ladies' heads.

"The big rain is coming!" said all the ladies. Mam jumped up and pushed some papers into a box. She took the blankets down from the roof poles and pushed them into the box too.

"I think I should run home quickly," said the lady with the baby. "I don't want the baby to get cold and wet." Off she went with the baby bobbing up and down in its sling on her back.

"Maybe we should all run home," said another lady. But it was too late. *Pat pat pat*, the rain was falling in big drops on the roof of the house.

They all looked up at the grass roof. It was a good roof. No rain would come through. But suddenly, *Whoosh!* a section of the grass roof at the very top was blown off in a strong gust of wind. There was a big hole in the roof! The sky far above was a browny-grey colour.

Plat plat plat, the rain came heavier now. Some of the rain didn't stop at the grass roof. It came right on down through the hole and fell on the ladies' books in the middle of the room.

Maki's mum know what to do. She ran to Mam's fireplace. There was a torn-up cardboard carton there. She grabbed it and said, "Quick, Maki, climb onto my shoulders."

Maki climbed onto his mum's shoulders. Mum held his ankles. Maki stood up straight. He took hold of the pole above his head and pulled himself up onto it. Just like climbing a tree, he thought.

Then his mum passed the cardboard to him. "Push it in the roof where the hole is," she said. Maki wedged the cardboard into the sides of the hole. As soon as it was fixed in place, the rain could not come inside any more.

"Tomorrow Maki's dad will come and mend the hole properly with new grass," said Maki's mum.

"Thank you," said Mam.

Now it was very dark outside, and inside too. The rain was falling heavily. Almost like standing under a waterfall, Maki thought.

"It's too dark to see!" said the ladies. "We can't have the class any more today."

"What we can do," said Mam, "is to pray for the people in other places. The big rain doesn't do much real damage here. But in other places it is even bigger. A real storm. The storm will knock people's houses right down to the ground. Let us pray that God will keep the people safe in this storm."

So all the ladies and Mam, and Maki too, prayed that God would keep the people safe in the storm. Soon the big rain stopped. The browny-grey clouds went away. All the ladies went home to their own houses. Maki and his mum went home too.

THURSDAY

Maki saw someone hopping along the path. It was Kirinda.

"Kirinda, why are you hopping like that?" he asked.
Kirinda was Sami's older sister. She was usually busy
with the jobs that big girls do. She carried water. She
collected wood. She took care of Sami and Tanga and
Maki. But today she was hopping along the path.

"I'm hopping because I can't walk," said Kirinda.
"My foot is swollen and hurting. I'm going to Mam's to
get medicine."

Maki went along with her. When they reached Mam's
house, Kirinda showed the place on her foot where a sharp
piece of wood had made a deep hole in the skin. All her
foot had gone red and swollen.

Mam got a green plastic basin. She filled it with water.
Then she put a tiny drop of purple medicine into the
water. The water turned pink.

"Now put your whole foot in here," said Mam. "We'll
let it soak for a while."

Just then Sami came running down the path.
"Kirinda, quick!" he yelled. "Mum says you have to go
home right away."

"I can't," said Kirinda. "My foot is soaking in medicine."

"No! I mean, go! Oh, I mean, don't not go!" Poor
Sami, he was excited and muddled up all at once. Kirinda

didn't move at all.

"Kirinda! The secret is happening!" he yelled at his sister again.

This time she did move. "The secret? Wow!" she said. She pulled her foot out of the basin and jumped up. Medicine spilled on the floor. "Sorry, Mam, I've got to go!" she said. She went hopping away home as fast as she could.

Mam wiped up the medicine that had spilled on the floor. She looked puzzled.

"Why did Kirinda need to rush away so fast?" Maki asked Sami.

"It's because of the secret," said Sami. "Shall I tell you?"

"Tell us!" said Maki.

"Well," said Sami, "The baby is being born right

now." He made his voice quiet when he said it. Then he added, "Granny is already at the house helping."

Maki's eyes opened wide. "Wow!" he said. Mam stayed quiet.

Sami told them some more. "It has been growing inside mum's tummy and now it is coming out to join us in the world. That's what 'being born' means."

"Wow!" said Maki again. "It's exciting." He gazed at his friend Sami. He wished he was Sami, having a new baby born into his family. He had been too small to remember when Tanga was born.

"Kirinda has to warm up water and cook extra food. They always do things like that when babies are born," said Sami.

"Do they?" said Maki. He was surprised how much older Sami seemed when he said all these things that his mum had told him.

Then Mam the missionary spoke. "You boys stay here at my house for a while," she said. "Sami's mum and granny won't want any noise when the baby is coming."

Then Sami had a question to ask Mam. "Are babies born in your country the same as they are here?" he wanted to know.

"Yes, sure they are!" said Mam. "Except that sometimes in our country the mum goes to hospital when it is time for the baby to be born. Then if it is hard for the baby to come out of her tummy, the doctors and nurses in the hospital help."

The children thought for a while about Mam's answer. Then Maki said, "I'm glad I didn't have to go all the way to a hospital to be born."

"Me too!" said Sami. "It's much easier to be born at home with only granny helping."

Mam smiled. "But in our country the hospitals are close by. Not like here, where they are very far away."

After a while, Mam said they could go to Sami's house. She went along too. Sure enough, the new baby had been born. Sami's mum was lying on the sleeping mat. Granny had wrapped the baby in a cloth. It was next to mum on the mat.

"We've got a new baby!" shouted Sami.

"Hush!" said granny. "You'll frighten him with all that noise."

"Is it a him, granny? Is it really a boy?" asked Sami. He saw granny's eyes go up in the way that means yes.

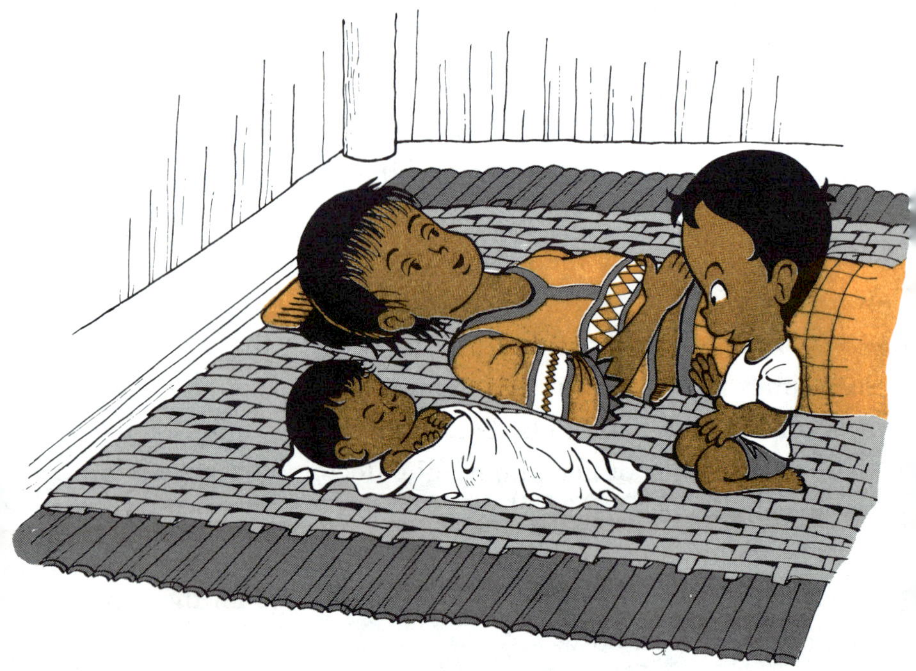

"I've got a new brother! A new brother!" He held tight onto Maki's arm and they both jumped up and down with excitement.

Soon Sami's dad arrived back at the house. He had just killed a chicken. He sat on the steps outside and began to pull the feathers off the chicken's body. He talked to Mam.

"Before you missionaries came here," he said, "we were always frightened of the bad spirits. Especially when a new baby was born, we were scared. We killed chickens to please the bad spirits, so they wouldn't harm the new baby."

"But now we know God will take care of the baby, and its mum," said granny. She had come outside to hear what they were saying.

"Why do we still kill chickens then?" asked a little voice. It was Maki again.

"Well," said Sami's dad, "we kill them for the mum to eat."

"Good food like chicken will help her to get strong again. It makes milk inside her body too for the baby to drink," said granny.

"I think we should say a prayer," said Mam. "We'll thank God that the baby was born safely."

"Pray for my foot to get better soon too!" called Kirinda from inside the fireplace.

So they all stopped their jobs. Sami's dad said a thank you prayer for the baby. Then Mam said an asking prayer for Kirinda's foot. Then everyone said "Amen." Maki and Sami knew that "Amen" is a special prayer word that means, "We agree." They both said "Amen" loudly too.

FRIDAY

It was bright and sunny again. Maki's mum was busy. She piled up all the clothes and wrapped them in a blanket.

"I'm going to do a big wash at the river today," she said. "I'll wash things for Sami's mum too now that the new baby has been born. You children can come too and take a bath."

"Tanga bat!" said Tanga.

"Oh good!" said Maki. "I'll be able to jump and splash in the deep pool."

Mum balanced the blanket bundle on her head. "Now we are ready to go," she said. "Maki, will you carry the bar of soap for me?"

Off they went down the path to the river. Maki carried the big bar of blue soap. Soon they reached the stones at the river side. The water was very clear and clean. Maki could see the big stones further down the river. He knew there was a deep pool there, and could hardly wait to run and jump in.

"Maki, you rub soap on Tanga while I am busy dipping these clothes and the blanket in the water," said mum.

"Aw, mum," said Maki. "I want to have fun jumping in the deep pool."

"Not yet," said mum. "I need you to look after your

little sister first. Come on now. Bath Tanga, then yourself.
It's fun getting soapy too."

So Maki started to rub soap on Tanga. When he had
finished, he let her sit in the water. She pretended to wash
her own dress, just like mum was doing.

Then Maki saw his friend Sami coming down the path.
"Hey, Sami!" he called, "Come and play!"

Sami ran down to join Maki, and both of them got all
soapy. Then they lay in the water with only their soapy
heads showing. They began to sing the song they had
learnt at church on Sunday:

"Who made the shining sun? God did.

Who made the running water? God did."

Suddenly they heard a crying sound. Tanga must be in
trouble! They sat up quickly and looked around. Mum
looked up too from her laundry work. Tanga was still
sitting in the river.

"Des, des!" cried Tanga. Mum saw what had happened. Tanga had let go of her new red dress and now it was floating away down the river.

"Catch Tanga's dress! It's floating away!" she shouted.

Maki saw the dress. It was going quickly towards the deep pool. Maki ran down the side of the river. Then he jumped onto the big stones. Then he jumped into the deep pool. Splash! He was just in time to grab the dress.

"I got it!" he called, and waved the dress above his head.

"Hooray!" shouted Sami.

"Good boy," said mum. Tanga stopped crying and started to laugh. They were all glad that the new red dress was safe.

Soon mum had finished the laundry work. "Come on Tanga, let's go home now," she said. "We will hang all this washing on the new fence. It will soon be dry in the bright sun."

"Can we go jumping in the deep pool now?" asked Maki.

"Yes, go and play there now," said mum.

Off went Maki and Sami to the big stones. "Me first!" shouted Sami. He jumped with a big splash. Then Maki jumped too. He sat down right next to Sami in the deep pool.

"Splash!" went the water. "Splash!" shouted Maki. Then they climbed out onto the big stones and jumped again. "Splash!" Sami jumped. "Splash!" Maki jumped.

They kept on climbing out and jumping in and splashing and laughing. It was such fun. After a while they sat on the big stones to take a rest. They started to sing again:

"Who made the shining sun? God did.

Who made the running water? God did."

It seemed as though the song had been made specially
for singing at the river. Then they sang some new words
in the song:

"Who made jumping boys? God did."

They liked the new words in the song. They sang their
song over and over again.

"Let's go home now," said Maki. "We can sing the
new words to mum and Tanga. We can sing the new
words to your mum and the new baby too. I think they'll
all like the song, don't you?"

SATURDAY

'"La da ah la," sang Kirinda. "Does that tune sound right, mum?" she asked. Tomorrow it would be her turn to lead the singing in church.

"Yes, it sounds fine to me," said her mum. "It's good that you are practising the songs here at home. That way I can hear them too."

"Yes, you won't be able to go up to the church tomorrow," said granny. "You need to rest for a few days more."

Sami's mum sat up on the sleeping mat. She rocked the baby in his sling.

"Hurry now, Kirinda, and wash the breakfast plates," said granny. "We have lots of things to do today. There is always lots to do on Saturdays. On Saturdays we get ready for Sundays."

Maki's mum was coming up the steps into Sami's house. "That's right," she said. "We have lots of things to do today."

"Why, what will we do?" asked Maki. He came into Sami's house too.

"Well, as for me, I will dig potatoes like I do every day," said his mum. "But today I'll dig twice as many as usual. Some for today and some for tomorrow."

"I will come with you and dig potatoes for our family,"

said Kirinda. "My foot is better now. It's not red or swollen or hurting any more."

"She is good at digging potatoes," said granny. "But how will she carry enough for two days? The basket will be too heavy for her."

"I'll go too and help carry," said Maki. They all smiled at Maki. He always tried to be helpful.

"It's better for you to stay here," said Maki's mum. "The slopes of the potato fields are very slippery."

"It rained last night," said Kirinda. "The mud at the

bottom of the slopes will be very sticky."

"The basket of potatoes will be very heavy," granny added. "Your mum won't be able to carry you too."

"Aw, I'm big now!" said Maki. "I won't slip on the slopes. I won't stick in the mud. And I can carry all the potatoes that I'll eat! Then mum's basket won't be so heavy."

Just then Maki's dad and Juni came into the house too.

"You know, Maki," said his dad, "I think I will be the one to go with your mum and Kirinda today. There is a special job for you boys to do here."

Then Maki's dad explained that they needed firewood. "Enough for two days, not just one. Enough for two families, not just one. After all, how will we eat the potatoes if there is no firewood to cook them with?" he said.

So that's what they did. Maki's mum and dad and
Kirinda went off up the path towards the potato fields.
Granny stayed at home taking care of Sami's mum, the
new baby and Tanga. Juni, Sami and Maki began to do
their special job.

They went towards the river to find wood. Juni carried
a knife in one hand. Sami dragged his mum's basket along
behind him as he followed Juni. Maki ran in front looking
from side to side in the grass.

"What are you looking for?" called Sami. "Is there a
snake in the grass?"

Maki smiled. What if there were a snake? That would
be fun!

"I'm looking for wood, of course," he told Sami.

"We'll go to the river side," said Juni. "There is plenty
of wood there. Small pieces, easy for you small kids
to collect."

"We can pretend to hunt for snakes too," said Maki.
"It will be a good game."

Soon they reached the stones at the river side. There
was lots of wood on the stones. It had blown off trees or
floated on the water when the big rain had flooded the
river. Maki and Sami ran about, picking up branches and
twigs. Maki picked up a long thin twig.

"Here's a long wriggly snake!" he said.

Sami picked up a shorter piece of branch. "Here's a
short fat snake!" he said.

They threw their snakes into a pile near the basket.
Juni chopped some bigger pieces of wood with his knife.
Then he pushed the wood into the basket until it was
tightly packed.

"We'll take this wood to our house," said Juni. "Then we'll come back for another basketful for Sami's family." That is what they did.

When they had finished they felt tired and hungry. Granny was pleased with the children's work. She roasted some cobs of corn, one for each of them to eat.

Later Maki's mum and dad and Kirinda arrived back too. They were also tired and hungry. Granny roasted more cobs of corn for them to eat.

Maki remembered what granny had said earlier, "On Saturdays we get ready for Sundays." He wanted to ask granny what it meant.

"Why do we get ready for Sundays on Saturdays?" he asked her.

"Sunday is a special day now that we are Christians," said granny. "We don't do our normal work on Sundays. It is the day when we take a rest. On Sundays we worship."

"What does 'worship' mean?" asked Maki.

"It means being glad about God. About who He is and what He has done for us."

"Like me," said Kirinda. "I'm pleased I'm the one to lead the singing tomorrow. This week there have been so many things that I'm thankful to God about. The new baby being born safely, and now my foot is better too."

"We can be glad about God every day, can't we?" asked Maki.

"Yes," said granny, "but on Sunday we give Him our time too. We go to church and learn more about Him, and about how He wants us to live."

SUNDAY

Maki's dad had something small and wriggling in his
hands. It was a pig with ginger hair. He had just brought
it home. Maki was excited when he saw the pig. He
watched his dad carefully. Dad tied a string around the
pig's neck. Then he tied the other end of the string to one
of the posts underneath their house.

"We must keep him tied up," said Maki's dad, "so that
he cannot stray and eat vegetables."

Maki stroked the small pig on its back.

"May I look after him, dad?" he asked.

"Yes, that's a good idea!" said Maki's dad. "You can
call the pig your own. You must bring him food every day."

Maki was excited about that. He felt very big. "Dad
must not think that I am just a little kid any more," he
thought. "Looking after a pig is an important job!"

"Come inside now." It was his mum calling from up
inside the house. "It's Sunday today and we are all going
to church."

Maki climbed up the ladder that reached from the
ground to the doorway of their house. He went inside.
His dad followed him.

"Put on your clean yellow shirt," said mum. She was
dressing Tanga in her new red dress. Soon the whole
family was ready to go. They climbed out of the house and

started out along the path to church. The path was narrow, so they walked in a line behind each other. Dad and Juni went first, then mum and Tanga. Maki was last in the line.

Suddenly Maki remembered something. The pig! Maybe he would feel lonely at the house with everyone gone. Maki decided to take the pig to church. After all, the pig was part of the family now! Maki ran back and untied the string from the post of the house. Then he gave it a quick tug. The small ginger pig trotted along behind Maki. Off they went along the path to church.

Soon Maki saw someone ahead of him on the path. It was Mam the missionary. He ran fast to catch up with her. The string pulled on the small pig's neck, making the pig run fast too.

"Hello, Mam Linda!" Maki called out as he ran. He hoped she would notice the pig. He was proud of his new pig, and she was the first person to see him with it.

"Hello, Maki," said Mam. "Oh, you have a pig with you! Is he new?"

"Yes, he's new," said Maki. "Dad says I can call him my own. I'll look after him and feed him every day."

"Where are you taking him now?" asked Mam.

"Why, to church, of course," said Maki.

"Oh, I see!" said Mam, smiling.

Maki went ahead on the path and hurried up the steep slope to the church. He walked inside and up to the front of the benches with the pig.

"Maki, you can't bring the pig to church!" It was his mum's voice again, and she sounded very strict.

"Aw, mum," said Maki. "He might be lonely at the house with everyone gone."

"Ig, Ig ...." said Tanga. She liked the pig too and wanted to reach out and touch him. Mum held her tight on her lap.

"No, we can't have any 'igs' in church," she said. "Take him outside and tie him at the corner."

Poor Maki, he did look sad. He led the pig outside and tied him up at the corner pole of the church. He patted the pig's head, and then went inside again. He sat on the bench next to his dad and Juni.

Soon it was time for the service to begin. Kirinda got up to lead the singing. She sang the first line of a song. Then all the people joined in and sang too. They knew the songs by heart. Maki knew some of them. He sang as loud as he could. He liked singing.

Then Sami's dad got up and started to talk. All the people were listening. Maki was listening too, but after a while he thought of something else he wanted to do. He saw Sami on a different bench. He slid down under his own bench and crawled to where Sami was.

"Come on, let's go outside," he whispered. Sami slid down under his bench too and they both scrambled between the legs of the people until they were outside the church.

"Come see my new pig," said Maki. "He's tied at the corner."

They went to where Maki had tied the pig. But the pig was not there any more!

"Oh, no! My pig is gone!" said Maki. "Where can he be?"

The two boys looked all round the sides of the church. The pig wasn't there. They looked behind the bushes, but the pig wasn't hiding there. They looked down the path towards the village, but the pig wasn't down there. They looked behind the stalks of corn, but the pig wasn't there either.

"My new little pig is lost!" said Maki. "The only one I ever had, and now he's lost." Poor Maki, he felt so sad that he began to cry.

Sami didn't like it when Maki began to cry.

"Come on, let's go tell your mum," he said.

Back inside the church they went and squeezed between the legs of the people again. They reached the bench where Maki's family were sitting. Maki's mum looked surprised when she saw the tears on Maki's face.

"What's wrong?" she asked.

"Maki's pig is lost!" said Sami.

"Yes," said Maki. "He's lost. He's not there any more, where I tied him."

"We looked everywhere," added Sami.

Maki's dad and Juni heard what the two boys said.

"Maybe he ran down the side of the hill. He might even fall in the river!" said Juni. When Maki thought of his new pig falling in the river, he started to cry all over again.

The people who were reading their Bible books stopped reading. They looked up from their books to see who was crying. They saw Maki.

"What is wrong?" they asked Maki's mum and dad.

"Maki's pig is lost," said his mum and dad. Then all the people started to talk. Everyone wondered where Maki's pig could be.

Then Sami's dad had an idea.

"We had better pray for the pig," he said. "I'm sure God knows where the pig is. God can make him go home safely. Let's ask Mam Linda to pray for Maki's pig."

So Mam stood up to pray and all the people closed their eyes to pray too.

"Dear God, we don't know where Maki's little pig is, but You do. Please make him go home safely to the house." That was the prayer. The children were pleased when they heard the prayer. Maki sniffed and pulled up his yellow shirt till it reached his nose and eyes. He wiped away his tears. Then he sat down quietly next to his mum and Tanga.

When the service was finished, all the people started to go down the path in a long line towards the village. Maki and Sami ran ahead very fast. They could hardly wait to see if God had answered the prayer and sent the pig home.

When they reached Maki's home, they looked under the house. Sure enough, there was the small ginger pig. He was lying fast asleep in the shade.

"He did come home! He did come home!" shouted Maki.

"He's not lost any more!" said Sami. They jumped up and down and ran to tell their mums and dads. Then they ran to tell Mam the missionary too. Everyone was happy that God had answered their prayer, even a prayer about a lost pig.